IN ART WE TRUST

FoA

THE FUTURE of your ART

A journey out of the jungle

H.S. DENKE
powered by LOUVRE ACADEMY

•

CONTENT

The Future Of Your Art

The artist way can sometimes seem like a trail through the jungle. Obstacles, confusion and the lack of a clear path are the things that make our artistic future uncertain. After having stayed in the jungle for too long, we can lose our way or just give up. Although this is true, however, we often forget how easy it is for some things to make their way through the thickest jungle to end up in something bigger. We forget how a river forms a path through the jungle. The water just follows naturally its own intuitive laws. Just like the flow of your creativity, the water is finding and exploring a way out. To get out of the jungle, all we have to do is to follow this flow. All you need is a vessel and some resources to stand through this journey. With this exercise, you will attain such a vessel to follow your flow of creativity to a bigger and better future.

Outstanding and aesthetic art can only be achieved when the artist focuses his mind 100% on it. Most creative artists work so hard on their art to the extent that they rarely ask themselves,

"What do I believe to achieve as an artist and what kind of artist do I hope to become?"

In this way, nagging worry about the future of your art is taking away your focus on being the outstanding artist you can be.

If you think, “I am not sure if my art has any future at all”, stop to worry. About the two factors that really can stop your future have been taken care off. Our experience has shown that it comes down to two simple obstacles that have to be managed. Most creative artists fail just because of two factors; they can’t find paying clients to support their work; and/or there is no enduring vision behind their art to convince clients and stand through the years of convincing the market. Just imagine for a moment that those two things have been taken care of and you can now focus on the future of your art. Once your future is clear enough, ways to fix these challenges will open to you.

It is time to ask yourself about your ideal artistic future. What type of artist do you want to become? What artistic skills would you want and need to reach? What interactions and cooperation would you want to have?
With these questions and reflections, you will discover more direction in your creative progress and career. You can focus more on your art and become less worried about the vagueness of your artistic future. The goal is to recognize what you could do today to venture into the artistic future you wanted to have.

From the beginning, this program is intended for the “creative.” It is effective at aligning thoughts with reality. It defines what artists want as a future for their arts, and helps to achieve it.

How does it Work? It's just so simple!

This Program is designed to help visualize a supreme future that is about 4 years from now on. How would your artistic life be? How could you set it up in such a way that would be best for your art? This program will guide you. It will make you consider what you have high regard for, how to improve, what skills to learn, what artistic career goals to set, how and where to improve as a person and your surroundings. Also: what and which artistic network you should choose and how to balance your art with life.

This program has as well a creative part, which involves expressing yourself on your artistic future, and how to use your Creativity at its best. The program will help you with your ideal artistic future and assist you to prioritize your objective. You will be able to evaluate your personal and social impact as an artist. This program delivers a construct which can identify potential obstacles and strategize their solutions. It is a tool for your progress and will support the future of your art.

You will get out of "the jungle" by following your artistic flow. All you need do is to follow the 3 steps to building your vessel.

Let your journey begin! Start with the ASSESSMENT PART to discover your first ideas about your future.

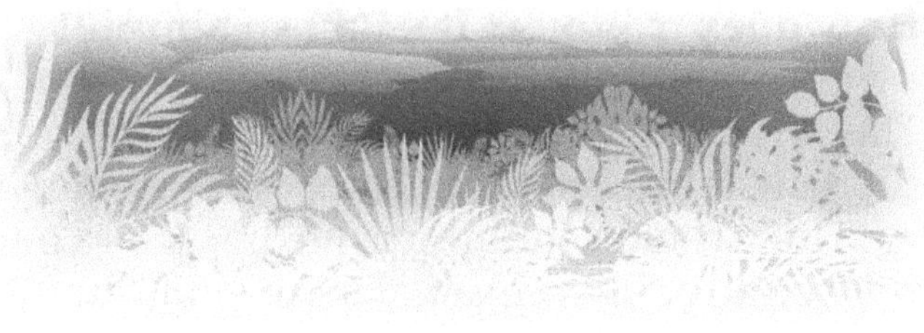

ASSESSMENT PART
The Future Of Your Art

The assessment part that follows after every chapter is effective at aligning first ideas with more thoughts and details.

Reading the following questions, write down and/or draw any ideas or spark that comes spontaneously into your mind. Express yourself about your ideal future, without criticism. Feel free to doodle and be creative. Often a drawing or a picture are saying more than 1000 words.
Imagine everything already has worked out! Visualize a supreme future that is about 4 years from now.

- How would your artistic life be?
- How could you set it up that would be best for your art?
- Consider what you have high regard for?
- How to improve, what skills to learn?
- What artistic career goals to set?
- How and where to improve as a person?
- How and where to improve your surroundings.
- What your artistic network to choose?
- How to balance your art with life?

MY FIRST IDEAS

THE EXPEDITION BEGINS!

Let's just begin your expedition out of the difficulties of your jungle, into the vast ocean of possibilities for your art in the future. The building of your vessel will, and can only begin with your creativity. You will have to express yourself about your artistic objectives and then point out the path of your river that you will follow. To assist you further, we will set your intentions to stay focused on your journey. This exercise has been designed to allow you to do an in-depth study of some of the virtues and imperfections of "you" as a creative. As the artist at your best, you will be able to discover the better future your art deserves.

This exercise has 3 easy steps;

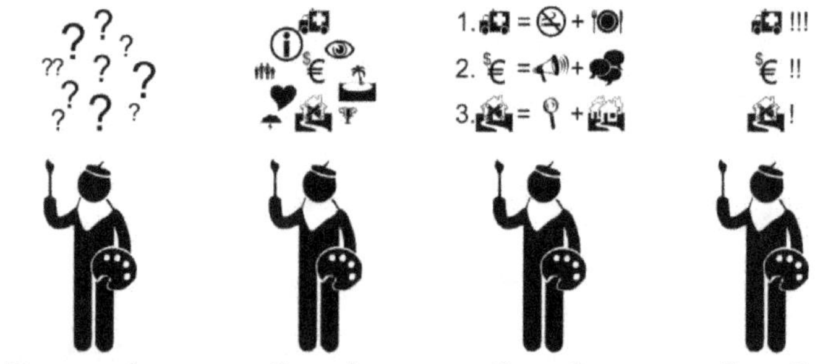

Preparation Step 1 Step 2 Step 3

Each will help you to find out more about yourself as a creative and the expedition beforehand. Like in every expedition, we will take some time of PREPARATION to understand your artistic flow and your hopes for the future.

STEP 1: You will write generally about your artistic objectives and the goals you intend to achieve.

STEP 2: You will specify and clarify the nature of those artistic objectives, and begin to strategize, so your future becomes clearer.

STEP 3: You will start your journey from here as you are now focused on what you really want from your future.

At the end of the 3 Steps, you will be able to create in your artistic notebook a clear outline of your future. Your sensible plan will help you to achieve strategic fix points in the years to come. You will be certain for what fix point you will set off. It will be possible for you to identify the first milestone you will achieve in the next week. Even down to know what you will do tomorrow and prepare it with a task you set yourself as attainable today. On the same day you finish the 3 steps the path to your artistic future will be clear. The precondition is to trust your art and follow through.

I recommend that you complete and repeat these three processes above over some days.

Feel free to start and stop whenever you like and take the necessary time. Creatives who allow themselves some time to express themselves fully, appear to do better and to benefit the more.

Take **STEP 1** and **STEP 2** separately from each other and let time pass to reconsider your inspirations. For **STEP 3**, I recommend an Artist Notebook that will capture in drawings and writing your journey as an artwork on its own.

Creativity and inspiration take time. The 3 Steps will focus and process what you are expressing and developing for your future. The questions are easy, but at the same time, it's a creative challenge with an artistic outcome. To achieve the best outcome do what you would do for your best artwork. Good results are achieved by stepping sometimes aside. Like taking a short break for a walk to return to your task afresh works wonders.

Your advantage in this process is your creativity. Try work from raw expression into detailed and fine appearance. Like a stonemason, cut out first big ideas, and then later on the fine details.

Start with liberated thinking about
Your Ideal Artistic Future.

The first exercises will jumpstart your imagination. After briefly answering these questions, you will be asked to draw or write for some minutes. Express yourself about your ideal future, without criticism; feel free to doodle and be creative. Often, a drawing is more spontaneous and significant.

Try to put yourself into a state of dream-like thinking. Set your internal imagery free. This mindset allows all your different internal states of motivation and emotion to express yourself in the best way. On the other hand, don't let your emotions, especially the negative one, overpower you. Take a break and relax if necessary. You are working at the essence of your art and nobody expects fast results from you.

It might be best to concentrate on your future for about a period of 4 years. Why 4 years? This is because we as humans often underestimate what outstanding achievements can be made in some years. Often we overestimate what we can achieve in 1 year and we forget how much we can accumulate over some years. You may have reasons to concentrate on a shorter or longer time span from 6 months to 8 years, and that's OK too.

Doing this exercise will make you develop a vessel for a better future for your art. The most important point is for you to believe in yourself and your art for the duration of this exercise. These are your thoughts and feelings you are expressing only for yourself. There is no judgment. Express yourself freely and draw or write non-stop. Try capture first the raw power of your mind, and then refine as much as you like. Try to be fertile with your thoughts as much as you can because it's all about the future of your art.

Let's start with discovering your foundation.

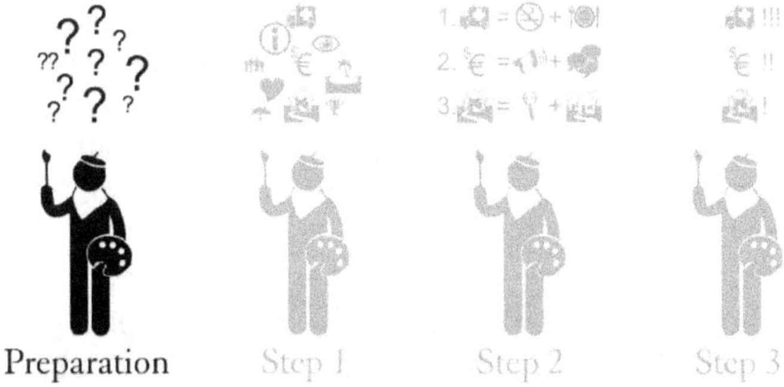

PREPARATION AND INITIAL THOUGHTS

Doing this exercise will help you develop a vehicle for a better future of your art. Give yourself the freedom and the fuel to enjoy this ride. Your mindset during the questions that follow should be open. For the time being, believe in yourself and a great future for your art. If there is a part of you that still worries about the factors why most creatives fall short, be calm. There are two links below; one will help you to find affluent clients for your artistic knowledge to support your work.

www.Client.Louvre.Academy

The other will help you develop a more convincing and enduring artistic vision to convince the market.

www.Vision.Louvre.Academy

(You can type this link in a web browser.)

BUT for now, just imagine for a moment that those two things have been taken care of already and you can focus on the future of your art.

Close your eyes and vividly picture your past artworks that made you feel good about yourself. Those moments when you were in great workflow and just creating on its own has given you a feeling of fulfilment. Perhaps there have been moments when you stepped back from your artwork and thought "this feels right for me." You have been in THE ZONE in which creative energy was just flowing through you. This ZONE is an important part of your art – it's your spark of genius. Take time to let this feeling sink in.

This feeling was the ground zero of your best art. You have been productive and brilliant. The moments of artistic greatness already exist in this ZONE. Let's now think about how we can get you more often in this flow. You have the choice to do it more constantly and better!

NOTE: To achieve the best outcome: Read the questions and exercises through. Think about them for a short time. Make a note or a quick drawing. After finishing a chapter, take time to revisit the question and explore the answers in more detail. You will find a Workbook section after each Chapter with plenty of space.

TIP: This is the time to start a new artist notebook just dedicated to your artistic future.

Write your thoughts down without any hesitation or self-censoring as they are.

A.0: Your Zone Of Genius and your creative flow at its best

Let's find out how to kick-start the zone of your artistic genius. Every artist has moments of genius - the work bits that just deliver the best he or she can offer. If you could choose only one precondition that supports you getting into the creative flow - THE ZONE - what would it be? A particular environment, mindset, knowledge or a routine? You can write down whatever the preconditions were so far and pick one that is always recurring in your mind.

A.1: One Thing You Could Do Better In Art

An artist is rarely satisfied with the artwork that is produced BUT there is the art you approve. Most likely made in THE ZONE: But what are the other artworks missing? If you could choose only one thing that you could do better to get your art to the next level, what would it be?

A.2: Things to Learn About Art

What would you love to learn more about what you are doing in art, in the next six months, 2 or 4 years?

A.3: Improve Your Habits and Art Routines

What creative habits would you like to improve on? What routines would boost your art?
For the sake of your inspiration?
For your expression?
For your art?
To get more often into YOUR ZONE by starting a special routine or habit?

A.4: Your Artistic Network in the Future

Your network is an important part of an impactful, productive art. Take a moment to consider your artistic and social network. Think about the corporations and the colleagues you might want to have, and what connections you might want to make. It is perfectly reasonable to choose associates who are good for your art. Describe your ideal artistic network life.

A.5: Your recreation for more artistic productivity

Take a moment to consider the activities you would like to pursue outside of obligations such as artistic work. The activities you choose should be worthwhile and personally meaningful to empower your art.

Without a plan, people often default to whatever is easiest, and this does not help to recreate their mind and body. An artist's mind should relax and be empowered to do what it is created for. This can only be counter-balanced through meaningful recreation.

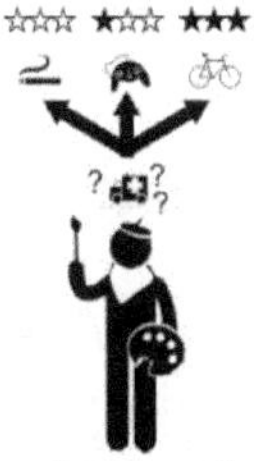

The content and value of your time as you develop should be the focal point of your recreation. Describe what your recreation life would be like if it was set up to be genuinely feeding your art and be enjoyable to you.

A.6: Your Art Fellowship in the Future.

Art should feel like a Home connected to a supporting group that cares. Take a moment to consider your Fellowship of other creatives, friends or family. What life provides you with a sense of meaning, belonging, and support for your ambitions? What kind of company, followers, partners would be good for you? How could you improve your relationship to move your art forward? Describe what your ideal Fellowship would be like.

A.7: Skills and Qualities You Admire In other Arts and Artists

Artists you automatically admire also have qualities that you would like to possess or imitate. Identifying those qualities can help you determine what it is that you can implement from them. Take a moment to think about the two or three artists you most admire. Who are they? What qualities do they possess that would also boost your art?

A.8: Your Artistic Career in the Future

An artistic career provides impact, security, status, and the possibility of contributing to the culture. Take a moment to consider your career so far. If you are to choose what art should provide for you in the future, what would be the goal? - would it be more of financial security, reputation, possibilities, skills/abilities, personal development that you expect?

Where would you want to be in the next 6 months? 2 years? 4 years? Why?

Is there an artistic Vision you are trying to accomplish?

A.9: Time for your artistic essence

I'm glad you've taken the time to think briefly about your artistic future, later we will have some time to consider more details. This step gives you the chance to integrate all the things that you have just thought and wrote about and to bring it down to an essence. At this stage make just small notes about the most important thoughts.

Be free and creative. Everything is possible. Close your eyes and daydream. Imagine your ideal artistic future.

- ✓ What kind of artist do you want to be?
- ✓ What do you want to do as an artist?
- ✓ Where do you want to end up with your art?
- ✓ Why do you want to achieve these things with your art?
- ✓ How do you plan to achieve your artistic goals?
- ✓ When will you put your plans into action?

Take a break and repeat each question in your mind. Make a note. Later take time to explore it more. Write down and draw the ideal future you have just imagined. Write continuously and do not stop while you are writing. Don't worry about being right or wrong - you will have an opportunity to perfect it later if you like.

Be creative enough, and Dream while you express yourself; don't stop. Create at least until 30 minutes have passed. Be brave and ambitious; everything is possible. Imagine a life that you would regard as artistic, creative and impactful. (You can use notes from visualizing a supreme future from the beginning.)

A.10 A Future to Avoid

You have now expressed the artistic future you would like to have. Having a defined future for artistic development increases your chances of experiencing positive growth. Pursuing a valued future will set a transformation free that benefits your art.

It can also be very useful to think of a future you would like to avoid. You probably know of artists who have made bad decisions. You can learn to avoid the death of your art from such people's experiences.

Use your imagination to motivate yourself to stay on your chosen path to the future. Draw on your knowledge of failure that you have experienced in the past. In this way, you'll stay true to yourself and your decisions.

Go beyond a simplification of a burned-out and penny-less artist without a vision. Draw a dark picture of what your life would be like if you failed to define or pursue your artistic future, because pain sometimes can be a source of motivation. This will stimulate you to stay on track. Take a mental picture of how your life would look like in 4 years, if you failed to stay true to your artistic progress.

This is the shadow of your life that you cast. Your shadow will remind you to stay out of it. You know where you don't want to be and you are ready to do whatever it takes so as not to end up there. Take your time until it is a future you want to avoid.

The expression of your imagination about the light you want to reach and the shadows you want to avoid should be expressive. Remember, you create only for yourself. Choose your goals that you want to pursue just for your own artistic reasons. Not because someone else thinks that those goals are good or important for a creative; you don't want to create someone else's art and life. Include your deepest feelings about all your artistic goals.

After having an insight into the vast ocean of possibilities and into the shadows of the jungle we want to avoid, we then can start. You are ready to take the first step into a brighter future and begin to build your vessel. Start the assessment.

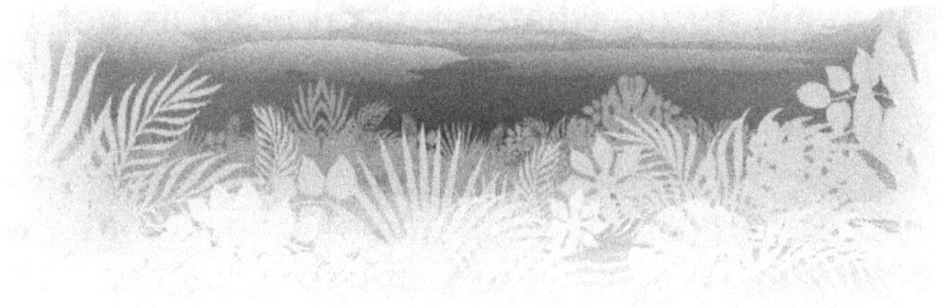

ASSESSMENT PREPARATION AND INITIAL THOUGHTS

Your mindset during the questions that follow should be open. Believe in yourself and a great future for your art.
Close your eyes and vividly picture your artworks that made you feel good about yourself. Pick one and describe it:

Describe the moments when you have been in great workflow and working alone has given you a feeling of fulfilment.

Describe the sensation when your art feels right for you:

Describe 3 points indicating you are in THE ZONE in which creative energy is flowing through you.

A.o.

Your Zone Of Genius and your creative flow at its best.

If you could choose only one precondition that supports you getting into the creative flow, THE ZONE what would it be?

A.1.

One Thing You Could Do Better In Art

There is your art you approve, most likely made in THE ZONE: What are the other artworks missing?

If you could choose only one thing that you could do better to get your art to the next level, what would it be?

A.2.

Things to Learn About Art

What would you like to learn more about what you are doing in art, in the next six months? 4 years?

A.3.

Improve Your Habits and Art Routines

What creative habits would you like to improve?

What routines would boost your art?

For the sake of your inspiration?

For your expression?

For your art?

To get more often into YOUR ZONE by starting a special routine or habit?

Your own Ideas:

A.4.

Your Artistic Network in the Future

Consider and describe your social network until now:

Describe the corporation's, colleges you might want to have.

What connections you might want to make.

Choose and describe associates who are good for your art.

Describe your ideal artistic network life.

A.5.

You recreation for more artistic productivity

Describe activities you would like to pursue outside of your artistic work.

Which and why some activities you choose would be worthwhile and personally meaningful to empower your art.

Describe your unhealthy and counterproductive recreation until now:

Describe why they are not really recreating for your mind and body.

How could something better healthier counterbalance those negative once as meaningful recreation.

Describe what your recreation life would be like if it was set up to be genuinely feeding your art and be enjoyable to you.

A.6.

Your Art Fellowship in the Future.

Which part of Art or art world feel like a Home for you connected to a supporting group that cares?

Consider and describe your Fellowship of other creatives, friends or family your home base so far.

What life provides you with a sense of meaning, belonging, support for your ambitions?

Describe what your ideal Fellowship would be like.

What kind of company, followers, partners would be good for you?

How could you improve your relationship to move your art forward?

A.7.

Skills And Qualities You Admire In Other Art and Artists

What artists do you always / automatically admire?

____

____

____

____

____

____

What qualities that you would like do they possess?

____

____

____

____

____

____

Which one could and would you like to imitate?

____

____

____

____

____

____

Identifying and describe those qualities / skills that can help you determine what it is that you can implement from them.

Take a moment to think about the artists you most admire. Who are they as a professional as a human?

Which qualities do they possess that would also boost your art?

A.8.

Your Artistic Career in the Future

Rate spontaneous (ZERO POINTS none at all, NINE POINTS most important) what an artistic future/ career should provide for you:

(0 to 9)
__ Impact on the world and others,
__Security,
__Reputation,
__Possibilities and opportunities,
__Skills/abilities,
__Status and significance,
__Contributing to the culture,
__ Personal development
__other:____________

Choose the highest ranking and describe what art should provide for you in the future what could be your goal.

____
____
____
____
____
____
____
____
____
____

Where do you want to be in 6 months?

In 2 years?

In 4 years?

What achievement, quality or goal will make you stay committed so long and why?

Is there an artistic Vision you are trying to accomplish? Is it motivating you for what you have described before?

A.9.
Time for your artistic essence

Integrate all the things that you have just thought and wrote about and to bring it down to an essence.
Read again through your notes and try to express it in only a few words. Imagine a life that you would regard as artistic, creative and impactful.

What artist do you want to be?

What do you want to do as an artist?

Where do you want to end up with your art?

Why do you want to achieve these things with your art?

How do you plan to achieve your artistic goals?

When will you put your plans into action?

Make a small drawing about the ideal future that you have just imagined for last minutes.

A.10
A Future to Avoid

Name and describe artists who have made bad decisions and destroyed their future in your opinion.

Why do you think did they made those decisions?

What bad decisions did you make for your own art so far?

From such artist and own experiences, what can you learn to avoid a decline in your art?

What motivates you most to stay out of such bad decisions and on your chosen path to your artistic future?

If possible, in one word: What would make you stay true to yourself and your decisions for a better future?

Draw a dark picture of what your life would be like if you failed to define or pursue your artistic future, which would motivate you with pain.

Describe your life in 4 years, if you failed to stay true to your artistic progress.

What would remind you to stay out of this dark future, every day? What visual trigger can you set?

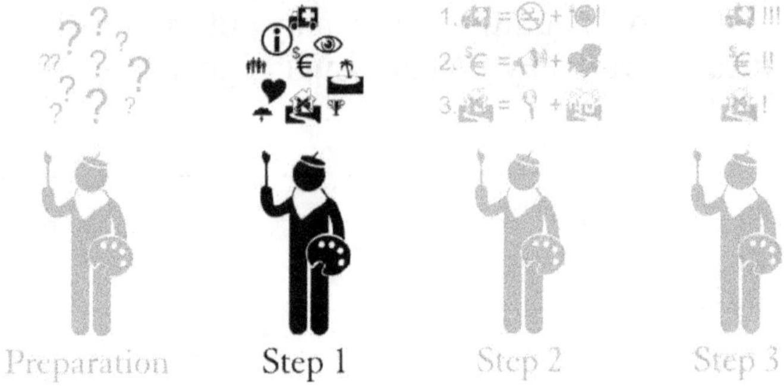

STEP 1
Building the future you want

In the PREPARATION you have now realized a glimpse of your ideal artistic future and outlined a future that is best avoided. You can put together a summary of the beginning of your journey to help you with a planning process.

TIP: If you encounter challenges in summing up all of your notes into brief memorable sentences, try to write in the third person. Start the sentence with "An artist with a great future will ..."

Again to achieve the best outcome, read the points first. Express yourself about the most important one. Then combine your ideas with the essence of your PREPARATION.

(Remember: Make only brief notes here. An assessment will follow this introduction. It will help you to summarize the essential points.)

The points that will help you plan are:

A.0. Your Zone of Genius and your creative flow at its best.

A.1. One Thing You Could Do Better

A.2. Things to Learn About

A.3. Improve Your Habits and Routines

A.4. Your Social Life in the Future

A.5. Your Recreation in the Future

A.6. Your Fellowship in the Future.

A.7. Skills and Qualities You Admire

A.8. Your Artistic Career in the Future

A.9. Your Artistic Essence

A.10 A Future to Avoid

These will be the seeds for your prosperous future. Remember in the planning not to stay in your comfort zone. What you write should not feel too easy but more like a challenge that you like to invite into your life for the sake of your art. It can be helpful to rewrite your first draft of your future plan until reading it provides you with a good feeling. It should be similar to what you feel when you are in the zone of your artistic flow. Don't worry if the manifesto of the future you want reads and feels a little bit bumpy, in the second step we will make a clear course out of it. If uncertainties are still creeping in your mind, just remember that a solution of the main 2 factors why creatives fail has been provided for you:

www.Client.Louvre.Academy

www.Vision.Louvre.Academy

Your art has potential just with your talent and the support of affluent clients and a stronger artistic vision to reach the outcome you want. So focus on your artistic future and let's set a course for you. Your future is not a threat it is your best promise to your art.

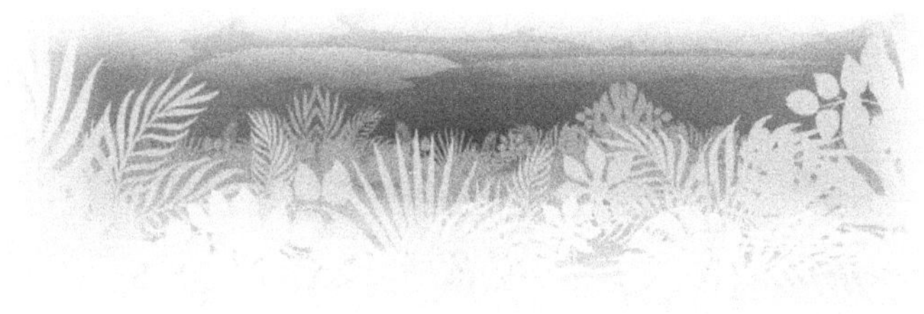

ASSESSMENT
STEP 1
Building the future you want

Put a summary of the beginning of your journey to help you with a planning process. Go through your notes and try to summarise the main essential points. Be brief, an essential one sentence is much better to become a mantra for your future.

TIP: Again, if you have problems, to sum up, your plenty of notes into brief memorable sentences, try to write it in the third person. Start the sentence with: "An artist with a great future will ... "

A.0. Your Zone Of Genius and your creative flow at its best.

____

____

A.1. One Thing You Could Do Better

____

A.2. Things to Learn About

A.3. Improve Your Habits and Routines

A.4. Your Social Life in the Future

A.5. Your Recreation in the Future

A.6. Your Fellowship in the Future.

A.7. Skills And Qualities You Admire

A.8. Your Artistic Career in the Future

A.9. Your Artistic Essence

A.10 A Future to Avoid

What point or goal until now is in your opinion very challenging for you? And why?

To which challenge are you looking forward to, because you know it is worth for the sake of your artistic growth? And why?

FIRST OUTLINE: outline Put the points together to one text. Rewrite your first draft until reading it provides you with a good feeling. It should be similar to what you feel when you are in the zone of your artistic flow. Try to summarise only the most important points that you consider vital and doable for your future?

All done? Congratulations! Now it is time to get on board and set your course.

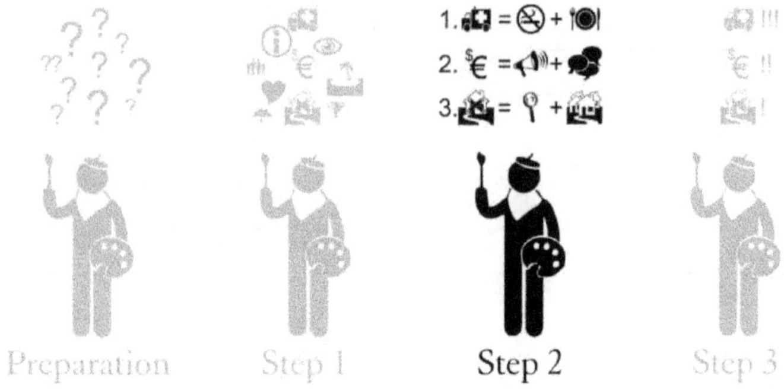

STEP 2
Setting the course

"Wishing without execution is nothing but a delusion, and to follow delusions in the jungle is deadly."

Let us layout some fix points of your future as a clear path. First, we will identify what point will make the largest impact on your future as an artist. In this way, you will define a fix point. It is like climbing on the highest palm to see the ocean on the horizon to set it as a direction to walk forward to. After this introduction reconsider your previous essential points in the assessment that will follow.

B.1: The Essence of Your Ideal Future

Read your Summary again and try to imagine a vivid picture of this future. Begin perhaps by writing "The Perfect Future of My Art" and if your summary is in the third person, switch it from *"An artist with a great future will ..."* to *"As an artist with a great future I will ..."*

Write down the Factors that will make your art flourish. Be inspired by the last summery but add what is essential, more details and factors to your highest artistic outcome. Perhaps it is a bigger studio, stronger vision, freedom or source of inspiration or you want affluent clients. Write down such necessary realistic points to achieve.

B.2: Prioritizing Your Fix Points

Take a look at the realistic points and factors you have written down. Some of them are real items, situations to achieve, or important points to accomplish. If you have written down a list of the most important points, then try to judge how important/impactful every point is, to realize your artistic future.

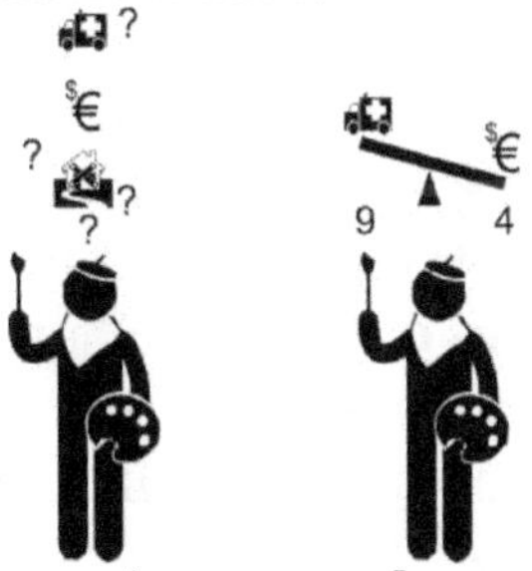

The easiest way is to evaluate it like in a competition. Each Fix Point is a candidate performing value for your artistic future. As a judge of this contest you can evaluate 0 (ZERO) points for candidates that will underperform. On the other hand give up to 9 (NINE) points if the Fix Point will have great value for your future. Trust your gut feeling in judgment! You can make your own system of jugging but the easiest one is to set in front **a ZERO POINTS** for none at all or **NINE POINTS** if the point would lead you and would have a very positive impact on your artistic future.

*For an example: The Fix Point candidate of a "bigger studio proposal" is not so trendsetting and important right now, so that's just **4 POINTS** for this candidate. BUT the next Fix Point to get a "stronger vision for my art", that's **9 POINTS** for this candidate. You have made this decision because a stronger vision even with a smaller studio will produce better art in the future. In this way of evaluating you can develop a hierarchy even in a bigger list of the ideas for your future.*

Try to pinpoint a factor that has the highest positive influence with the least amount of effort or resources. If you have no candidates with **9 POINTS** take time to think again what is important to your art. If you have too many Fix Points with **9 POINTS** up front make a decision to set only for the extraordinary **10 POINTS** (If so then only in front of three of them.)

B.3: Specifying and Clarifying Your Goals

Underline now 3 most impactful points. Don't worry you can re-judge, re-write and organize

later. It is also OK to pick up to 6 Fix Points if they are absolutely essential, but try to focus on a narrow doable path. It is useful to take chewable chunks one at a time.
Become very specific about the chosen points. Clarify and write down for every of the underlined points what you exactly want to achieve and the steps that are necessary.

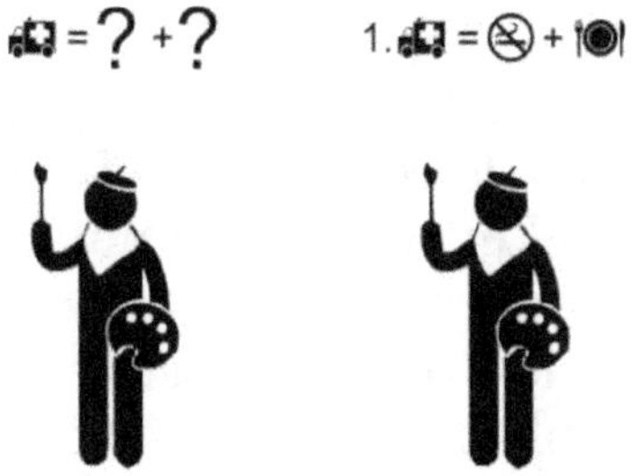

TIP: If you don't know what to write and you're unmotivated to do so, check if this Fix Point that you set out for your future is really so important for your art or just an illusion. Follow your gut feeling and try other points that are not underlined to check if you are more motivated.

You can start vague and become more and more specific about "the how', like:

"I would like to be focused on my art, in this and that way....."

For example: Your career goal might be "I would like to be more interested in my art market, by exploring this possibility...."

Or: about your impact like "I would like to influence more people with my art or vision, by …".

Or: about what you value "The future of my art is worth it to..."

Make the specifics as focused as you can. Each Fix Point should contain clear objectives.

For example: Fix Point health and energy for your art. It should contain the obvious objective to give up smoking and better nutrition to boost your artistic energy. Make the chosen points motivational for you as possible so you don't have any problem telling it to yourself in 2 to 3 sentences in front of a mirror. Like: "The future of my art is worth it to become healthier by giving up smoking and eating well."

Now that we have a course, let's make your course more stable. The plan we have developed so far can be perhaps overwhelming. But try to look beyond this overwhelm. Remember you have a course. So with the 2 readymade solutions (www.Client.Louvre.Academy and www.Vision.Louvre.Academy) you're already on the way. Your outlook into a brighter future with affluent clients and a stronger artistic vision is enough BUT let's go a step further and develop your motivation to go all the way. Star the assessment to write it all down, make it clear and set your course in more detail.

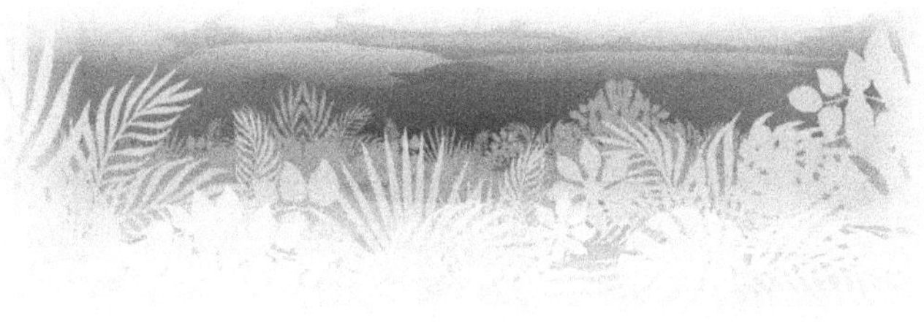

ASSESSMENT
STEP 2
Setting the course

Go back to the FIRST OUTLINE from Step 1. Identify and underline in your text what point will make the largest impact on your future as an artist. (Favour the one that includes or describes realistic objects or situations).
Set visual fix-points of your outline for a visualisation. List the realistic objects or situations that will appear in your future like you would list stage settings or props for a play or movie.

1 ____________________
2 ____________________
3 ____________________
4 ____________________
5 ____________________
6 ____________________
7 ____________________
8 ____________________
9

B.1.

The Essence Of Your Ideal Future

Read your FIRST OUTLINE again and the list of your props and stage sets. Try to imagine a vivid picture of this future as you would imagine a film scene. Name the film "The Perfect Future Of My Art" and if your summary is in the third person switch it from "An artist with a great future will ... " to "As an artist with a great future I will ... ". Write a synopsis of this movie or what would be on the back side of a book describing your 4 years of you as an artist on your way to your success.

The Perfect Future Of My Art

Underline the most vital props, situations or set pieces in this synopsis. List them below:

1 ______________________________
2 ______________________________
3 ______________________________
4 ______________________________
5 ______________________________
6

Are those factors that will make your art flourish in the future? What would transform or boost them into something that would bring you to your ZONE of artistic genius? Rewrite the list into an optimum of clear Fix Points with details that will make you be more often in your ZONE of artistic genius.

1 ______________________________
2 ______________________________
3 ______________________________
4 ______________________________
5 ______________________________
6

B.2.

Prioritizing Your Fix Points

Before you proceed: If still a little unclear to you; try to transform your Fix Points into real items, situations to achieve or important points to accomplish.

Let's evaluate your Fix Points. It is easier to prioritize them when you think for a moment why you are achieving some things easier than others. What strengths, qualities or factors did the process of achievement involved in the past so it was easy for you to get what you want? (Achievement process involving returning outstanding abilities or strengths of you, like planning, communicating or empathy and so on.) List some of your strengths that are making achievement for you easier:

____

____

____

____

____

Considering now one of your Fix Points you can estimate now if the achievement process is down the line of your strength or not.

Judge now how important/impactful is every Fix Point is and how doable it will most likely be for you.
The easiest way is to set in front a 0 for none at all or a 9 if the point would lead you and would

have a very positive impact on your artistic future. Keep also in mind that the achievement process should also involve some of your strength.

MY FIX POINT	Future impact and doable (0 TO 9)
1	
2	
3	
4	
5	
6	

For example: A bigger studio not so important right and it does not involve any of my strength. I hate searching. Only 4 points.
To get a stronger vision for my art a 9, because a stronger vision even with the smaller studio will produce better art in the future and being creative and far-sighted is something that I love to do.

Underline 3 Fix Point that has the highest score, positive future influence with the least amount of effort or resources.

B.3.

Specifying and Clarifying Your Goals

Reconsider your underlined 3 most impactful Fix Points. Can anything be changed so that achieving them would bring you even more in the ZONE make it more impactful?
What element of achieving the Fix Point could be dropped? What part postponed so that it is more likely to realise it and you are more motivated to go through the process?

1 FIX POINT:

Add for ZONE:

Doable by removing:

2 FIX POINT:

Add for ZONE:

Doable by removing:

3 FIX POINT:

Add for ZONE:

Doable by removing:

Become very specific about the chosen points. Clarify and Write down to every of the underlined points what exactly you want to achieve and the steps or milestones that are necessary.

TIP: If you don't know what to right and are unmotivated to do so, check if this point is really so important for your art or just an illusion.
Follow your gut feeling and try other even not underlined points to check if you are more motivated.
Make the specifics as focused and motivational for you as possible. In a way that you don't have any problem telling it to yourself in 2 to 3 sentences in front of a mirror.

1 FIX POINT:

1 step to achieve it would be:

2 step to achieve it would be:

3 step to achieve it would be:

2 FIX POINT:

1 step to achieve it would be:

2 step to achieve it would be:

3 step to achieve it would be:

3 FIX POINT:

1 step to achieve it would be:

2 step to achieve it would be:

3 step to achieve it would be:

Some of the Fix Points contain more and harder steps than the other. Start with the most doable for you. Look at your Fix points and set them in a sequence I, II , III.
Try always to look beyond overwhelm.
Remember you have now a course for your Future, let´s start your journey now.

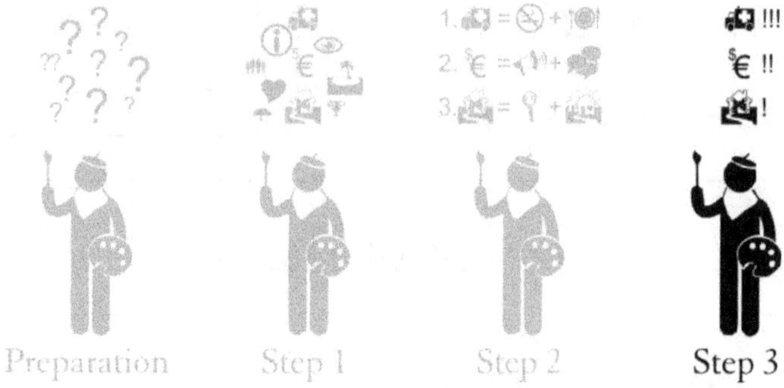

STEP 3
The Journey

"Make your artistic future count."

Your course will become now your journey. Now you will be asked about the following elements for each of the specific objectives you have set. This are the specific features that followed from the Fix Points you have identified and underlined before. It is important to rethink your **Motives**, evaluate your **Impact**, and think about the **Details**. Also obstacles should be considered. A clear solution for them will secure your future steps to progress. For example if you Fix Point was getting a healthier to boost your artistic energy, one of the important objectives is to give up smoking or get a high performing artist brain (www.Brain.Louvre.Academy). Knowing such clear solutions will make your journey easier.

Take each objective in the assessment that will follow and one by one rethink it under those points:

C.1.Evaluating Your Motives
C.2.Considering the Impact of artistic objectives
C.3.Considering the Strategies
C.4.Identifying Potential Obstacles and their Solutions
C.5. Progress
C.6. Steps to Future

By considering these points you know in advance how likely you will follow through or if you should choose perhaps another artistic objective. The best plan can fall apart without knowing yourself a little bit better.

For example: The objective of giving up smoking does involve the strategy of breaking your unhealthy habit. This sounds simple and great BUT this habit of smoking is part of your worrying pattern. Money trouble, for example, makes you grab a cigarette without you noticing it and this pattern can be hard to break. After the consideration you know that you first have to stop worrying about money by getting clients and then you are able to deal with the smoking habit. Some of the objectives even go deeper, that's why your planning is set out for 4 years to give you time. It is all about getting to the root of a problem.
Let me interduce how deep some of the problems of my clients can go:

A client knows that for his future he needs affluent clients. A clear and easy objective with the right help, but he has found out that he fears the success. Strange isn´t it? He fears what his current peer group might think of him. In this way, he knows in advance that a change of his vision towards success is needed to break free from his judgmental peers. The roots of the problem are the people and some of his beliefs that prevent his artistic future. It is wise to work on this root first.
To achieve a sustainable plan one has to go deep BUT be aware some of the objectives can become "a rabbit hole" without an end. If an objective becomes too complex it is wiser to refocus on a goal that is doable but still impactful. My experience has shown that by solving one or two of the fix points the one that was "an unsolvable rabbit hole" finds often a solution on its own.

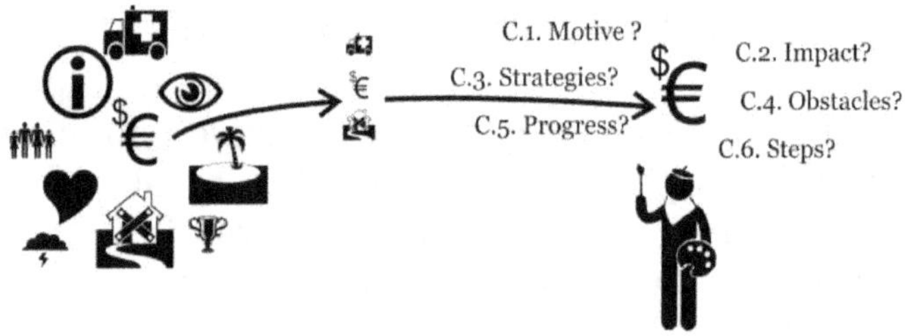

Take your most important Fix Point. Pick from it one of the key objectives that are a precondition to achieving this it. Consider the Fix Point in the assessment that will follow under these perspectives:

C.1: Evaluating Your Motives

Your motives for a goal are critical. For such a goal, you might want to consider your issues. The following can be:

Do you truly believe that pursuing this artistic objective is important for your art? (Or are you beginning an undertaking that let you drift away from being an artist?)

Do you want to achieve this artistic objective personally, or are you just doing it to please someone else? (In art it is often a good thing to do something for someone else, but you should know when you are doing that.)

Are you pursuing this artistic objective because the situation you find yourself in seems to demand it?

Is the pursuit of this artistic objective inspiring, stimulating or just satisfying?

Is this artistic objective part of a deeply-felt vision?

Please spend a minute or two writing down your reasons for pursuing this objective.

C.2: Considering the Impact of Goals

Setting out paths can have an impact beyond the obvious. Our specific personal goals are connected to the larger, more important vision.

These higher-order objectives reflect our most important artistic ideals. The specific artistic objective of spending more time studying is pointing to a higher goal. It is a specific element of the more important artistic objective of becoming a masterful artist.

Explore higher ideas affected by your attainment of the artistic objective like:

How would this affect the way your audience or others perceive you? (You might also consider fears of being successful.)

How would attaining this artistic objective affect the lives of the people around you?

What broader beneficial cultural impact might your success have?

Please write a short description of it (how attaining this artistic objective would change additional important aspects of your life, and the lives of others).

C.3: Considering the Detailed Strategies for Goal Attainment

Big objectives at once are hard, but when broken down to Milestones, they are easier to achieve. They are fundamental to reaching our greater ideas. To achieve them, strategies and routines are necessary. Often the breaking of a bad habit can become a good strategy for your progress. Consider what specific things need to be done in order to achieve your goals. Create practical strategies for realizing your dreams. Please take some time to write about the concrete daily or weekly habits and routines you might do to further your goal. Point out if an objective has the danger of becoming a "rabbit hole" of endless problems.

C.4: Identifying Potential Obstacles and their Solutions

Great art is a challenge; it is good that it is not too easy, otherwise everyone would do it. And so far, thinking about achieving an artistic objective is obviously easier than going out and getting it done. Many things related to the surrounding environment, the social situation, and self, all can block your path. It is useful to predict these difficulties to prepare ahead. Example: Big income trough your art is about finding clients and convicting them.

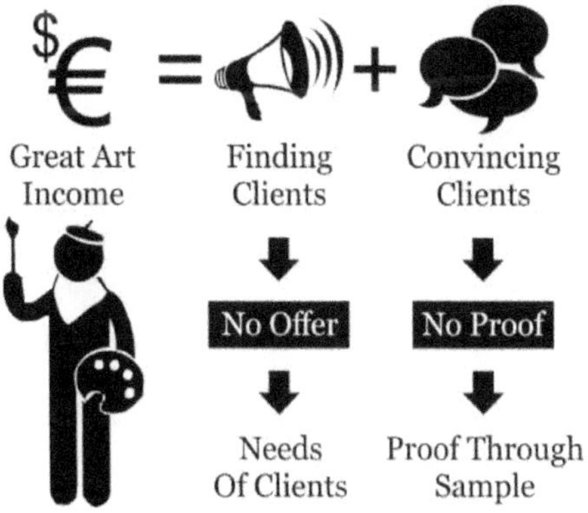

But to do this you have to offer something and proof that it is their money worth. Your

Potential Obstacles are to know what your client wants to get there interest and proof to them that you can deliver on their needs. Consider your objectives once again. Write down all the potential obstacles you can think of, and the ways to overcome those obstacles.

C.5: Progress

The path will remain only motivating when we see the progress. Look at the objective and the milestones and set the point at which you will know that you have achieved it. It can be as the end situation of the key to your new bigger studio in your hand. The written goals manifest to make your vision clear. It is only when you set a clear parameter that you will experience your success.

Ideas for setting such parameters of achievement:

When would you like to achieve this objective?

What is the evidence that you are progressing towards your goal?

How will things feel like so you are satisfied in your progress?

How can you find the balance between being too hard and being too soft on yourself?

C.6: Steps to the Future

Art is all about doing, not worrying. Do not worry about yourselves by constantly revisiting your progress. Just concentrate on realization. Never weaken yourself by questioning your intentions. Develop a natural flow to achievement. Instead of asking, "Am I doing the right thing?" Feel free to experiment. Worry is an unproductive behaviour which takes away the opportunity to learn and grow.

You have set objectives for a greater art, so concentrate on a daily implementation. It is the power of accumulation, which starts from the smallest step a day, which will take you forward on your path over a week.

Art is all about doing things even if they are not perfect. Experiments and implementation will automatically correct your path.

Get an artist's notebook just dedicated to your progress alone. Capture your progress, errors, and achievements in drawings and writing them down.

Tip: Van Gogh brother method. The struggle of an artist is a valuable expression that will inspire. Vincent van Gogh's life is so valuable to culture and inspirational because we have an inside in his fight for outstanding art. We have an inside since for Vincent it was a relief and self-assurance to express him freely in his letters to his brother Theo. This technique to write dedicated letters to even an imagined guardian provides a higher devotion to the task at hand.

Remember your path to a greater art is, in this way, already an authentic expression of yourself in this world. Your path out of the jungle into the vast ocean of possibilities is a work of art on its own. Let's map out your path with the following assessment.

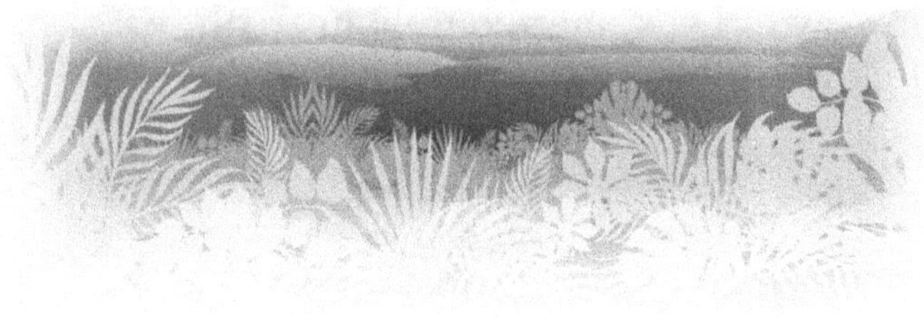

ASSESSMENT
STEP 3
The Journey

Reread the Fix Points and their steps. If necessary write them in a clearer form that will make the steps and the milestone to achieve stand clearly out.

If your Fix Points are too complex involving a difficult process of milestones, don't hesitate to evaluate each milestone under those aspects. By taking this step you know in advance how likely you will follow through or if you should choose perhaps another artistic objective.
Take each objective one by one and rethink it under those point of view:

C.1.

Evaluating Your Motives

For each Fix Point and/or Milestone that you will execute, you might want to consider issues such as the following:

- Do you truly believe that pursuing this artistic objective is important?
- Do you want to achieve this artistic objective personally, or are you doing it to please someone else?
- Are you pursuing this artistic objective because the situation that you find yourself in seems to demand it?
- Is the pursuit of this artistic objective inspiring, stimulating or satisfying?
- Is this artistic objective part of a deeply felt vision?

1 FIX POINT:

1 step:

2 step:

3 step:

2FIX POINT:

1 step:

2 step:

3 step:

3 FIX POINT:

1 step:

2 step:

3 step:

Please spend a minute or two writing down your reasons for pursuing this objective. Summarise your motive.

1 FIX POINT:

My Reason and motive in a nutshell:

2FIX POINT:

My Reason and motive in a nutshell:

3 FIX POINT:

My Reason and motive in a nutshell:

C.2.

Considering the Impact of Goals

Explore the impact beyond the obvious.
To what larger, more important part of your vision can your objectives be related or reflect your most important artistic ideals?
Explore higher ideas affected by your attainment of the artistic objective:

How would the success or achievement affect the way that audience or others perceive you? How would it change your self-perception? (You might also consider fears of being successful.)

1 FIX POINT:

The change of perception would be:

2FIX POINT:

The change of perception would be:

3 FIX POINT:

The change of perception would be:

How would attaining this artistic objective affect the lives of the people around you?

1 FIX POINT:

The change of my and other lives would be:

2FIX POINT:

The change of my and other lives would be:

3 FIX POINT:

The change of my and other lives would be:

What broader beneficial cultural impact might your success have? What would it change in a bigger picture of art?

1 FIX POINT:

The impact on culture and art would be:

2FIX POINT:

The impact on culture and art would be:

3 FIX POINT:

The impact on culture and art would be:

Please write a short description of it. How attaining this artistic objective would change additional important aspects of your life, and the lives of others.

1 FIX POINT:

The change of important aspects of my life, and the lives of others would be:

2FIX POINT:

The change of important aspects of my life, and the lives of others would be:

3 FIX POINT:

The change of important aspects of my life, and the lives of others would be:

Should you Fix Point involve impactful milestones, don't hesitate to ask those questions to each milestone or step that you plan to take.

C.3.

Considering the Detailed Strategies for Goal Attainment

Bigger objectives or steps should be broken down to more details. Reflect on your Fix Point and your Steps once more. Pick the one that contains a more complex achievement path and be more precise by describing it.

1 FIX POINT:

1 step:

2 step:

3 step:

2FIX POINT:

1 step:

2 step:

3 step:

3 FIX POINT:

1 step:

2 step:

3 step:

To achieve the Fix Points describe the overall strategies and routines that are necessary. Consider what specific things need to be done in order to achieve your goals. Create a more practical tactic for realizing them. Please take some time to write about the concrete daily or weekly habits, routines you might do to further your goal.

1 FIX POINT STRATEGY AND ROUTINE:

2FIX POINT STRATEGY AND ROUTINE:

3FIX POINT STRATEGY AND ROUTINE:

C.4.

Identifying Potential Obstacles and their Solutions

Describe briefly what overall difficulties you expect during the achievement of your Fix Points.

1 FIX POINT OVERALL DIFFICULTY:

____

____

____

____

2FIX POINT OVERALL DIFFICULTY:

____

____

____

____

3FIX POINT OVERALL DIFFICULTY:

____

____

____

____

Now that you have an overview consider more detail challenges. Write down all the potential obstacles you can think up. Write down ways to overcome these obstacles.

1 FIX POINT:

OBSTICLE:	SOLUTION:

2 FIX POINT:

OBSTICLE:	SOLUTION:

3FIX POINT:

OBSTICLE:	SOLUTION:

C.5.

Progress

The path will remain only motivating when we see the progress. Look at the objective and the milestones and set at what point you will know that you have achieved it. It can be as the end situation of: The key to your new bigger studio in your hand. The written manifest to make your vision clear. Whatever it is only when you set a clear parameter you will experience your success.

1 FIX POINT: ________________

When would you like to achieve this objective?

____

What evidence that you are progressing towards your goal?

____

____

How will things feel like so you are satisfied in your progress?

____

____

Other:

____

____

2FIX POINT: ________________

When would you like to achieve this objective?

____

What evidence that you are progressing towards your goal?

____

____

How will things feel like so you are satisfied in your progress?

____

____

Other:

____

____

3FIX POINT: ______________

When would you like to achieve this objective?

____

What evidence that you are progressing towards your goal?

____

____

How will things feel like so you are satisfied in your progress?

____

Other:

____

What positive mantra, visual trigger, or reminder can you set that you cannot ignore and will make you return to the progress for the sake of the future of your art:

____

If motivation through pain works for you: Go back to STEP 1 point <u>A.10 A Future to Avoid.</u> Find or create a visual reminder of this dark future prediction. What will it be, where will you place it to keep you motivated:

____

C.6.

Steps to Future

Art is about doing not worrying. Go to (C.3. Considering the Detailed Strategies for Goal Attainment) and pick one doable step or milestone.

Describe what you can do today to start the implementation.

Fix Point:

____

Milestone:

____

I will implement it do day by:

____

____

____

____

Describe what you will do tomorrow so even the smallest step today will bring you forward on your path.

____

____

____

____

Describe what you will do over the next week so it will accumulate to what achievement over this week.

Draw a small map of your plan like a river flowing through. It is passing points of achievements and draw also the troubles and challenges that can be expected on the journey

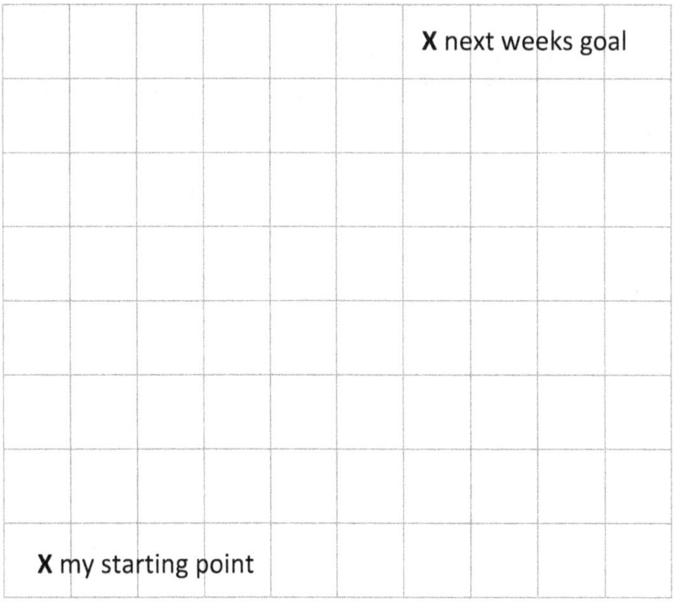

Reminder: If you didn´t so far. Start an artist notebook just dedicated to your progress. In drawings and writing capture your progress, errors and achievements.

START TODAY

You have developed a vessel to get to a better future of your art. It is now time to get in and enjoy the ride. Believe in yourself and the great future for your art. If there is a part of you that still worries and doubts if your vessel is strong enough, never you worry. You can build a strong artistic vision that will carry you through all the turmoil all the way through. You can use the wisdom of the old masters like Leonardo da Vinci on how to build and achieve your artistic vision. And if you worry about the resources for your long journey, then don't. Even now in your situation, you have the skills and knowledge to attract affluent clients that will fuel your journey. As earlier reiterated, there are two links below which will provide you with the most essential factors: affluent clients (www.Client.Louvre.Academy) and enduring artistic vision (www.Vision.Louvre.Academy). For everything you set out there is like for those two factors a solution. You are not the first artist to tackle the objectives, for most it has been taken care of already. Focus on the future of your art and start to work on a doable milestone today!

Start your first entry here that you will later transcript on the first page of your notebook:

The Future Of My Art

Today I took the first step for the future of my art that I will achieve in 4 years by setting out to complete these 3 points:

1 Fix Point:______________
2 Fix Point:______________
3 Fix Point:______________

First I will start with

(_) FIX POINT:

____

____

By taking on the first Milestone of:

(_) MILESTONE:

____

____

To prepare and make it happen I will this week achieve:

First week achievement:

____

To get the week started I will tomorrow already undertake the task of:

Tomorrow:

____

To prepare this task I will as an artist with a great future today...

Today's task:

____

I will break it down in these simple achievable measures:
1:____________________ finished at__:__
2:____________________ finished at__:__
3:____________________ finished at__:__

No matter what, describe today's first measure and complete it. This will generate momentum to stay true to your artistic future and tackle tomorrow's task. In the worst case; even when you can only take "baby steps" of 5 minutes a day they will accumulate over time. Keep in mind: In one day after tomorrow you will be working on your artistic future already for 3 days. 3 days nearer to the future you desire. Set yourself a challenge to work on your artistic future for 22 days straight. This time span creates automatically a habit and a routine that will keep you on track.

Congratulations on finishing this assessment and giving your art a profound future.

I hope you have enjoyed this exercise as much as I've enjoyed it putting all this together for you. The future is yours when you truly believe in your art.

www.ingramcontent.com/pod-product-compliance
Lightning Source LLC
Chambersburg PA
CBHW072157170526
45158CB00004BA/1684
* 9 7 8 1 0 8 2 5 7 9 5 3 0 *